	DATE DUE		

SOME MAJOR EVENTS IN WORLD WAR II

THE EUROPEAN THEATER

1939 SEPTEMBER—Germany invades Poland; Great Britain, France, Australia, & New Zealand declare war on Germany; Battle of the Atlantic begins. NOVEMBER—Russia invades Finland.

1940 APRIL—Germany invades Denmark & Norway. MAY—Germany invades Belgium, Luxembourg, & The Netherlands; British forces retreat to Dunkirk and escape to England. JUNE—Italy declares war on Britain & France; France surrenders to Germany. JULY—Battle of Britain begins. SEPTEMBER—Italy invades Egypt; Germany, Italy, & Japan form the Axis countries. OCTOBER—Italy invades Greece. NOVEMBER—Battle of Britain over. DECEMBER—Britain attacks Italy in North Africa.

1941 JANUARY—Allies take Tobruk. FEBRUARY—Rommel arrives at Tripoli. APRIL—Germany invades Greece & Yugoslavia. JUNE—Allies are in Syria; Germany invades Russia. JULY—Russia joins Allies. AUGUST—Germans capture Kiev. OCTOBER—Germany reaches Moscow. DECEMBER—Germans retreat from Moscow; Japan attacks Pearl Harbor; United States enters war against Axis nations.

1942 MAY—first British bomber attack on Cologne. JUNE—Germans take Tobruk. SEPTEMBER—Battle of Stalingrad begins. OCTOBER—Battle of El Alamein begins. NOVEMBER—Allies recapture Tobruk; Russians counterattack at Stalingrad.

1943 JANUARY—Allies take Tripoli. FEBRUARY—German troops at Stalingrad surrender. APRIL—revolt of Warsaw Ghetto Jews begins. MAY—German and Italian resistance in North Africa is over; their troops surrender in Tunisia; Warsaw Ghetto revolt is put down by Germany. JULY—allies invade Sicily; Mussolini put in prison. SEPTEMBER—Allies land in Italy; Italians surrender; Germans occupy Rome; Mussolini rescued by Germany. OCTOBER—Allies capture Naples; Italy declares war on Germany. NOVEMBER—Russians recapture Kiev.

1944 JANUARY—Allies land at Anzio. JUNE—Rome falls to Allies; Allies land in Normandy (D-Day). JULY—assassination attempt on Hitler fails. AUGUST—Allies land in southern France. SEPTEMBER—Brussels freed. OCTOBER—Athens liberated. DECEMBER—Battle of the Bulge.

1945 JANUARY—Russians free Warsaw. FEBRUARY—Dresden bombed. APRIL—Americans take Belsen and Buchenwald concentration camps; Russians free Vienna; Russians take over Berlin; Mussolini killed; Hitler commits suicide. MAY—Germany surrenders; Goering captured.

THE PACIFIC THEATER

1940 SEPTEMBER—Japan joins Axis nations Germany & Italy.

1941 APRIL—Russia & Japan sign neutrality pact. DECEMBER—Japanese launch attacks against Pearl Harbor, Hong Kong, the Philippines, & Malaya; United States and Allied nations declare war on Japan; China declares war on Japan, Germany, & Italy; Japan takes over Guam, Wake Island, & Hong Kong; Japan attacks Burma.

1942 JANUARY—Japan takes over Manila; Japan invades Dutch East Indies. FEBRUARY—Japan takes over Singapore; Battle of the Java Sea. APRIL—Japanese overrun Bataan. MAY—Japan takes Mandalay; Allied forces in Philippines surrender to Japan; Japan takes Corregidor; Battle of the Coral Sea. JUNE—Battle of Midway; Japan occupies Aleutian Islands. AUGUST—United States invades Guadalcanal in the Solomon Islands.

1943 FEBRUARY—Guadalcanal taken by U.S. Marines. MARCH—Japanese begin to retreat in China. APRIL—Yamamoto shot down by U.S. Air Force. MAY—U.S. troops take Aleutian Islands back from Japan. JUNE—Allied troops land in New Guinea. NOVEMBER—U.S. Marines invade Bougainville & Tarawa.

1944 FEBRUARY—Truk liberated. JUNE—Saipan attacked by United States. JULY—battle for Guam begins. OCTOBER—U.S. troops invade Philippines; Battle of Leyte Gulf won by Allies.

1945 JANUARY—Luzon taken; Burma Road won back. MARCH—Iwo Jima freed. APRIL—Okinawa attacked by U.S. troops; President Franklin Roosevelt dies; Harry S. Truman becomes president. JUNE—United States takes Okinawa. AUGUST—atomic bomb dropped on Hiroshima; Russia declares war on Japan; atomic bomb dropped on Nagasaki. SEPTEMBER—Japan surrenders.

WORLD AT WAR

Battle of Britain

WORLD AT WAR

Battle of Britain

By G.C. Skipper

CHILDRENS PRESS, CHICAGO

Hitler, Goering, and other high-ranking German officers at the Reich Chancellery.

FRONTISPIECE:
London rescue workers battle fires
started during Nazi air attack

Library of Congress Cataloging in Publication Data

Skipper, G.C.
  The battle of Britain.
  (His World at war)
  SUMMARY: Discusses the prolonged bombing of
England by the Luftwaffe in 1940, the tactical errors
made by the Germans, and the implications of the
outcome of the battle.
  1. Britain, Battle of, 1940—Juvenile literature.
[1. Britain, Battle of, 1940. 2. World War, 1939-
1945—Aerial operations] I. Title. II. Series.
D756.5.B7S55   940.54'21   80-15187
ISBN 0-516-04781-7

PROJECT EDITOR:
Joan Downing

CREATIVE DIRECTOR:
Margrit Fiddle

PICTURE CREDITS:
UPI: Cover, pages 4, 6, 9, 11, 13, 20, 21,
23, 27, 28, 29, 31, 35, 36, 38, 40, 45, 46
U.S. AIR FORCE: 8, 15, 16, 17, 18, 25, 33,
42
Len Meents: 37 (map)

COVER PHOTO:
London firemen at work on a fire started
by Nazi night-raid bombers

There was tension in the room. Jealousy seemed to crackle across the conference table.

Hermann Goering sat there in his Nazi uniform. He could feel the hostility of the others at the table—those in the German army and navy. Yet he had never felt more confident of his air force, the Luftwaffe. He was sure it could pave the way for the Nazi land and sea invasion of Britain. The invasion had been given the code name Operation Sea Lion.

It was August 1940. Goering shifted his huge body at the table. He felt a trickle of perspiration make its way down the very center of his back.

Adolf Hitler sat at one end of the table. He said nothing. His eyes, quick and darting, followed every word of the discussion.

"Why only last month you tried to draw the British into an air fight," an army officer was saying to Goering. "The Luftwaffe increased its bombing attacks on the English Channel and on all the southern ports of Britain. Is that not correct?"

"Ja," Goering replied.

These British Spitfires are ready for combat.

"And is it not also correct that the Luftwaffe failed? The Royal Air Force refused to be drawn into an air battle. What makes you think this plan—Operation Eagle or whatever it's called—will succeed?"

"Mein Fuehrer!" Goering said suddenly, frustrated. He turned toward Hitler. "There is nothing complicated about Operation Eagle. Please hear me out." He heaved his fat body up out of the chair. He totally ignored the army officer who had criticized him.

With one look, Hitler brought silence to the conference table. Then he turned his attention to Goering and waited for him to speak.

"We are all agreed on one point," said Goering. "The Royal Air Force must be crippled. Otherwise German army and navy troops will not be able to invade Britain successfully. Consider this: At this moment Field Marshal Kesselring's division is ready in the Low Countries and in northern France. Also in northern France is Field Marshal Sperrle. General Stumpff is awaiting my order in Norway and Denmark. Kesselring and Stumpff together have a total of 929 fighters, 875 bombers, and 316 dive bombers."

While Goering was making his plans to cripple the Royal Air Force, British aircraft plants were turning out warplanes at the rate of a thousand a month.

Goering paused to let this sink in. Then he looked at the conference table. He said, "I can assure you of this: Whatever British fighters are defending southern England can be destroyed within four days. Give me two to four weeks and I can not only cripple the entire Royal Air Force, I can wipe them out completely!"

"You also think the Luftwaffe, all by itself, can bring all of Britain to her knees," the army officer said sarcastically. His remark caused some laughter at the table.

"See here! My personal feelings are not the issue," Goering cried. "Operation Eagle is the topic of discussion."

"Quiet, both of you!" Hitler commanded. "I've heard enough. When can you launch Operation Eagle?" he asked Goering.

"We can start August 12. The entire operation will be underway no later than August 15."

For a moment Hitler stared steadily at Goering. Then he said, "I'm sure you will succeed."

For a moment Goering felt a touch of fear. But it vanished quickly beneath his sudden feeling of elation. Now, he thought, the Luftwaffe can prove itself once and for all!

"Ja, Mein Fuehrer!" Goering said, snapping to attention.

But Hitler had already turned his back on the conference table. He was leaving the room.

In the days that followed, Goering had much to do. He contacted Kesselring, Sperrle, and General Stumpff. He contacted all the other officers who would set the wheels of Operation Eagle in motion.

Hitler and Goering

And on August 12, just as Goering had promised Hitler, the Luftwaffe took to the air. Hundreds of planes lifted off from German airfields. Within hours, they swept across the borders and into the British countryside.

Machine-gun fire erupted. The whine of bombs filled the air. The Nazi planes hit the British with sudden, devastating power.

The British sent up their own Royal Air Force (RAF). Anti-aircraft guns roared upward toward the Germans. But the huge number of Nazi planes continued to sweep down. On August 12 alone the Nazis hit five British radar stations and destroyed another one.

During the next two days—August 13 and 14—the Germans threw 1,500 aircraft at the British. But when the air fight was over the scorecard looked surprisingly good for the RAF. The Luftwaffe had lost 47 planes. The RAF had lost only 13.

London headlines on August 13, 1940, tell of the devastating air raid conducted by the Germans the night before.

Goering had used an awesome number of Nazi aircraft. But he considered the first few days of air attack as only the warmup period. He had greater plans for the stubborn British. He had been waiting a long time for August 15. When it came, he gave the order that launched Operation Eagle full force.

"Tell Kesselring and Sperrle and General Stumpff that I want them to throw everything they have into the attack. We will wipe out the RAF in short order!" Goering commanded.

Goering's enthusiasm and confidence were catching. It filtered down to the men fighting under his command. On August 15 the first great sky battles took place. A total of 801 bombers and 1,149 Nazi fighters roared through the sky. They were headed for southern England. The world had never seen anything like it before. At the same time, about 100 German bombers roared along toward Tyneside, in northern England. They were escorted by 34 ME-110s.

This German fighter plane barely escaped Allied bombs.

The Germans in the north hit hard and fast. They far outnumbered the Royal Air Force defenses. Yet when the Nazis collided with the English, it was as if the Luftwaffe had run into a buzz saw. Without warning, almost as the Nazis neared Tyneside, the Germans ran into seven squadrons of British Hurricanes and Spitfires.

The British aircraft seemed to be everywhere at once. They screamed in from all sides. Their machine guns yak-yakked and spit scorching bullets into the Nazi planes. The ME-110s, acting as escorts, were riddled by the British. The bombers were now exposed.

British Spitfires over England fly to meet the oncoming Luftwaffe planes.

Above: A British fighter escort

Below: This captured German ME-110 is the same type of escort plane destroyed by the RAF near Tyneside.

The British, for their protection, put their
own insignia on captured German planes such
as these before flying them to bases in England.

The RAF moved in. Their tailgunners caught the Nazi aircraft in their sights.

The sky filled with the noise of screaming engines. The cries of wounded crewmen and pilots were swallowed up in the engine noise and gunfire. The Hurricanes and Spitfires lived up to their names. They criss-crossed General Stumpff's forces with bullets. The Nazis seemed as helpless as sitting ducks. The seven squadrons of RAF planes finally circled and soared up and away from the fight. Very little was left of the Germans. The RAF had knocked 30 Nazi planes out of the air. The others were hightailing it back to safety.

That one vicious air battle wound up most of General Stumpff's part in the Battle of Britain.

Meanwhile, the Germans were having better luck in southern England. The 800 German bombers were attacking the southern coast. There the massive attacks by the Nazis hit the British hard. The stream of German planes seemed to be

A shore battery observation post in England.

Hurricane fighters come in from battle to refuel and load more ammunition. This picture was taken while fighting was actually in progress against the gigantic Nazi air raids of August, 1940.

endless. More and more planes kept coming. They drove deeper and deeper into the British countryside. One of these attacks came very, very close to reaching London itself.

Like the deadly point of a spear, the Nazis swept in. They moved hard and fast. They knocked out four aircraft factories at Croydon. They damaged five fighter fields where RAF planes were launched.

The British were stunned. Further attacks on southern England would be disastrous. There seemed to be no way to stop the Luftwaffe.

But during this time, the unexpected happened. Goering made the first of two tactical errors.

Goering had no idea how vital Britain's radar network was. The Germans were still behind in developing radar. It did not occur to Goering that the use of radar was the reason the RAF, though outnumbered, had been able to put up such a fight.

The British sat still and watched their radar screens. When the blips came they knew exactly where the German planes were. It was a simple

LOOSE TALK CAN

CAUSE THIS

KOEHLER
ANCONA

This is the Enemy

1778 1943

AMERICANS
WILL ALWAYS FIGHT FOR LIBERTY

The British showed great courage during the
Battle of Britain. These American war
posters, though produced only after the
United States entered the war, reflect
the anti-Nazi feelings of all the Allies.

23

matter of getting the Hurricanes and Spitfires to the location they were needed most.

But radar was new to war tactics during this time. Goering did not realize its significance. On August 12 the Germans had badly damaged the British radar network. But Goering didn't know that. As a matter of fact he said, "It is doubtful whether there is any point in continuing the attacks on radar stations since not one of those attacked has so far been put out of action."

That was his first major mistake in the Battle of Britain. When he stopped attacking radar stations, the British were able to repair the damage. They put the stations back in working order.

The British sector station was very important. This was an underground radiotelephone network.

The sector stations openly guided the Hurricanes and Spitfires during the battles. The Germans could hear the constant chatter of English coming in on their radios. But in the beginning they didn't know what it meant.

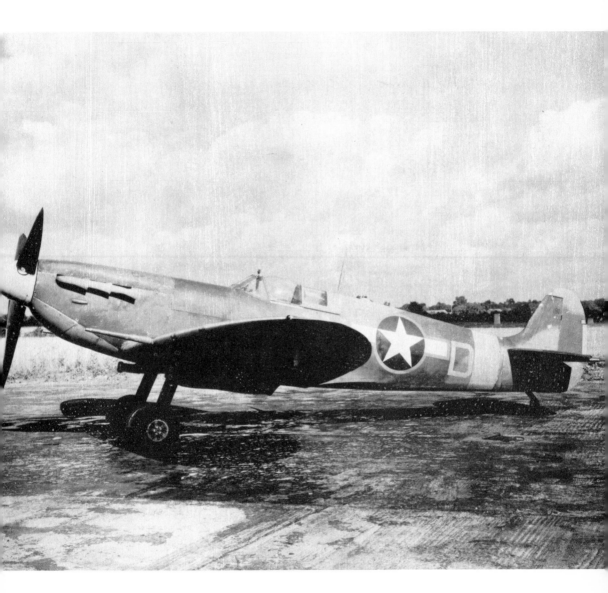

Closeup of a Spitfire parked on an airstrip somewhere in
England. The sector stations guided Spitfires during the
air battles against the Germans. The United States insignia
indicates that an American crew flew this plane later in the war.

As soon as the Nazis swept in, Hurricanes and Spitfires were zig-zagging all over the sky. They outwitted the Germans. They anticipated almost every move. The RAF was always one step ahead of the Nazis. And during all this air fighting the Germans had to listen to the irritating English voices in their ears.

Finally, the Nazis realized that what they were hearing played a significant role in the battle. On August 24 the Germans changed their fighting tactics. They zeroed in on the sector stations.

Seven sector stations were of major importance. They were located on airfields near London. Six of these were hit by the Germans. Suddenly the sound of English on the Nazi radios came less frequently.

Radar stations were damaged. Sector sections were damaged. Airfields were damaged. Britain was rapidly losing the Battle of Britain.

It was a frightening force that Germany threw at the English. During this time the Nazis launched

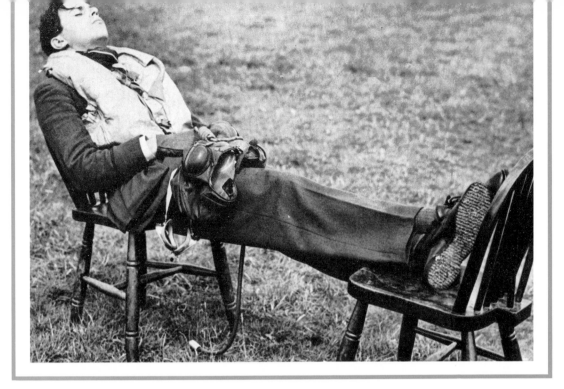

Exhausted RAF pilots had to rest whenever and wherever they had a chance.

an average of 1,000 planes a day. By sheer numbers they overwhelmed the British. They pushed the country to the very edge of total disaster.

Things were very, very bad for the British and they knew it. "Gentlemen," an English officer told a high-level staff meeting, "if the Nazis continue these attacks for a few more weeks we cannot withstand it. Britain will collapse."

The RAF pilots were exhausted. Defeat seemed certain. Nevertheless, the Royal Air Force continued to send every pilot and aircraft it had into the skies against the German onslaught.

Then a strange thing happened. It changed the entire shift of battle.

On August 24, a group of German bombers made a navigational error. It was a simple, mathematical mistake. But because of it, the Germans accidently bombed the center of London. Homes were blasted away. Civilians were killed.

This view of London shows one of the areas badly damaged by Nazi air raiders. In the center is St. Paul's Cathedral. Dome at extreme right is that of Old Bailey.

Left: A German bomb exploding in their home doesn't daunt W.O. England (left) and his brother C.R. England. Their slogan is from a popular English song of the time.

Below: "Pram Squad" children of London were allowed to collect firewood from damaged buildings.

The English were furious. They thought the Nazis had killed civilians on purpose. The RAF waited until night. Then they took off. Under cover of darkness, the RAF planes swept across the border. They dropped their bombs right into the center of Berlin.

Little damage was done. But the German people were stunned. For the first time ever the city of Berlin had been bombed.

The RAF were still outraged by the German bombing of London. They struck again at night on August 28 and August 29. This time German civilians in Berlin were killed.

The Germans reacted the same way the British had. The Nazis were furious. Not only had Berliners been killed, but the English night bombings had created another problem. Berliners were greatly disillusioned with the Nazi leaders. They were rapidly losing faith in the leadership. They wanted only one thing—peace.

Pilots (above) and gunner (below) of a four-engine heavy Stirling bomber are only three RAF men who took part in the bombing raids on Berlin.

Hitler had to do something. He couldn't let that public mood continue. It would be disastrous for his own ambitions. It would also be disastrous for the outcome of the war.

On September 4, Hitler addressed the German people. The entire tone of his speech was sarcastic. He made fun of Churchill. He made fun of Chamberlain and Eden. He made fun of other British leaders. He ridiculed them. He poked fun at them. The German people were delighted with the speech. And then Hitler threatened the British with the worst night bombings ever carried out.

Because of Hitler's promise, Goering made his second major mistake in the Battle of Britain. He changed his entire course of action. He stopped hitting the airfields and sector stations. Instead, he turned his attention to the city of London. During the late afternoon of September 7, German bombers attacked London with a vengeance.

Captured German planes at a Fighter Group base in England—
a JU-88 (above) and an FW-190 (below). The British put their
own insignia on the planes before flying them to home bases.

Shortly after eight o'clock that night, the second wave of Nazi planes came in. That night of September 7 the Germans threw 625 bombers and 648 fighters at Britain. In the first wave there were 320 bombers. They were escorted with every single fighter the Nazis had. They roared up the Thames and dropped bombs with horrendous force on English power stations. The bombs destroyed waterfront docks that stretched for miles. They blew up Woolwich Arsenal. They turned railway depots into piles of splinters. This attack lasted until four-thirty Sunday morning.

Then the Nazis pulled back. And waited.

At nightfall the Nazis were back again. They swarmed over Britain with 200 bombers. They went in and stayed. They unloaded their bombs all night. They ruined the countryside. During these first two nights of bombing, a total of 842 persons were killed and 2,347 were wounded.

Above: One of the battery of searchlights that penciled the skies nightly in search of Nazi raiders. Below: These men were part of the staff who guarded St. Paul's Cathedral in London during the night raids.

And the British had other problems, as well. The RAF pilots were exhausted. Between August 23 and September 6, 466 RAF fighters were either destroyed or badly damaged. The Germans had lost only 385 aircraft.

This air war had also taken another toll on the British. The battles killed 103 pilots and seriously wounded 128. This was one fourth of all the pilots they had.

British airmen exercise while recovering from battle wounds.

MAJOR BOMBINGS
BATTLE OF BRITAIN
JULY - NOVEMBER, 1940

SCOTLAND

Newcastle,
Tyneside

Liverpool

Hull

ENGLAND

Birmingham

Coventry

Ipswich

Bristol

London

Southhampton

Portsmouth

Plymouth

A six-year-old
London boy,
Freddy Harrison (left),
rescued his three-year-old
sister Winifred (right)
and baby sister
Joybell when a bomb
damaged their house
during a night raid.

The night attacks on London were awesome and nerve-wracking. But the RAF now had time to regroup. They could repair the damaged airfields and sector stations. They would be able to avoid disaster.

The German night assaults fell into a distinct pattern. They continued night after night for a solid week. At the end of the week Goering was elated. He was certain the night attacks had severely hurt Britain. No country could possibly survive that kind of pounding.

"Tomorrow morning," said Goering, "we will launch a fantastic daylight raid! They will never expect it!" Goering looked at the calendar. "We will throw everything we have at the British tomorrow morning. We will not wait for night." The date of the first daylight attack in a week was Sunday, September 15.

Crewman on a destroyer of the Dover Patrol scans the sea during his watch.

When dawn broke on that Sunday the early morning stillness was ripped apart. The noise was made by the engines of 200 German bombers lifting into the sky. Around them were 600 fighters. Their job was to escort the bombers to London. They were going to finish the business once and for all.

The sky turned almost dark with Nazi planes. The Germans moved across the English Channel. They banked and headed for London.

But the British still had their radar. It was in pretty good working condition by now. The RAF simply watched the Germans coming. They spotted the huge squadron of aircraft on the radar screen. They prepared for the attack.

Before the Germans even reached London, the RAF intercepted. They swarmed in and opened fire. The Germans were stunned.

Again, there were Spitfires and Hurricanes everywhere! Again, machine guns aimed with deadly certainty at the wall of Nazi planes. Bullets criss-crossed in a deadly pattern against the Nazi airplanes.

Most of the German planes had to scatter. Those that didn't leave the area were shot down. They went down screaming. They trailed huge plumes of black smoke. They crashed somewhere far below.

A captured German gliding bomb

Only a very few German planes made it all the way to London.

Two hours later the Germans sent in an even larger force of war planes. They hit with everything they had. But the RAF fought furiously and persistently. They pushed the Germans back again. They drove the attacking planes back to the safety of Germany.

Suddenly one thing was crystal clear to Hermann Goering. More importantly, it was clear to Adolf Hitler. This daylight failure proved something once and for all: The Luftwaffe no longer could carry out a successful daylight attack on Britain.

Two days later—on September 17—Adolph Hitler called off Operation Sea Lion—the invasion of Britain. Luftwaffe air attacks continued, however.

Early in November Nazi officers reported to a routine briefing session. An air of depression filled the conference room. Hitler took one look at the group. They were silent. They were not even bickering among themselves. Goering's huge body sat motionless at the conference table.

Hitler said, "From September 7 until November 3 the British endured 57 consecutive nights of bombing. Despite this pressure, they did not yield!" He stared at the conference table. Slowly his hand clenched into a tight fist, the knuckles growing white. "They did not yield," he repeated. "They did not yield!"

After the Battle of Britain, the Luftwaffe never recovered its losses. As an effective, powerful air force, it was destroyed.

Worst of all for the Nazis, however, was that Adolf Hitler had been stopped. It was the first time that had happened since the beginning of World War II. He would never look so invincible again.

A London woman smilingly rescues a fine plant from a home destroyed by German night raiders. Hitler was right. The British remained determined and cheerful throughout the Battle of Britain. They did not yield.

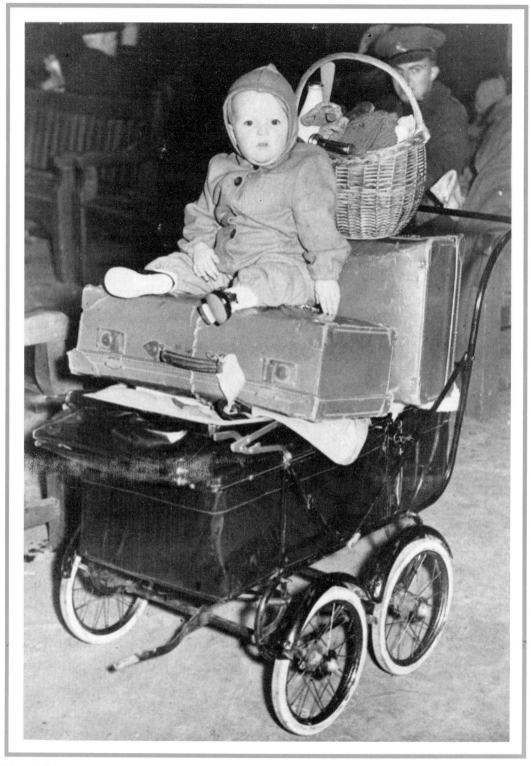

This child was one of thousands evacuated from London during the Battle of Britain.

INDEX

*Page numbers in boldface type
indicate illustrations*

About the Author

A native of Alabama, G.C. Skipper has traveled throughout the world, including Jamaica, Haiti, India, Argentina, the Bahamas, and Mexico. He has written several other children's books as well as an adult novel. Mr. Skipper has also published numerous articles in national magazines. He is now working on his second adult novel. Mr. Skipper and his family live in North Wales, Pennsylvania, a suburb of Philadelphia.